# Daily Positive Affirmations

## Handwriting Practice
## Write and Draw

Name

HARITAS
PUBLISHING

Name

 Daily Positive
Affirmations Drawing 

Write about one thing you like to do. Draw a picture of yourself doing what you like to do.

# Daily Positive Affirmations Handwriting Practice

I am perfect just the way I am.

**Let's Practice!**

# Daily Positive Affirmations Drawing

Draw a picture. Then write about your positive affirmation.

Name: ___________     Date: ___________

# ★ Daily Positive Affirmations ★
## Handwriting Practice

I love myself.

✏ Let's Practice! ✏

# Daily Positive
# Affirmations Drawing

Draw a picture. Then write about your positive affirmation.

# ★ Daily Positive Affirmations ★
## Handwriting Practice

I am smart and creative.

✏️ Let's Practice! ✏️

Name: _______________  Date: _______________

# Daily Positive
# Affirmations Drawing

Draw a picture. Then write about your positive affirmation.

# Daily Positive Affirmations Handwriting Practice

I am healthy and happy.

✏️ Let's Practice! ✏️

Name: _______________________     Date: _______________________

# Daily Positive
# Affirmations Drawing

Draw a picture. Then write about your positive affirmation.

Name: _______________        Date: _______________

# Daily Positive Affirmations
# Handwriting Practice

I am learning new
things each day.

✏ Let's Practice! ✏

# Daily Positive
# Affirmations Drawing

Draw a picture. Then write about your positive affirmation.

# ★ Daily Positive Affirmations ★
## Handwriting Practice

I am safe, loved, and protected.

✏️ Let's Practice! ✏️

# Daily Positive Affirmations Drawing

Draw a picture. Then write about your positive affirmation.

# Daily Positive Affirmations
# Handwriting Practice

I am a good friend.

Let's Practice!

# Daily Positive Affirmations Drawing

Draw a picture. Then write about your positive affirmation.

# ★ Daily Positive Affirmations ★
# Handwriting Practice

I am a good
listener.

✏ Let's Practice! ✏

# Daily Positive
# Affirmations Drawing

Draw a picture. Then write about your positive affirmation.

Name:                          Date:

# ★ Daily Positive Affirmations ★
## Handwriting Practice

I am enough.

✏️ Let's Practice! ✏️

# Daily Positive Affirmations Drawing

Draw a picture. Then write about your positive affirmation.

Name: _______________  Date: _______________

# ★ Daily Positive Affirmations ★
# Handwriting Practice

I am a fast learner.

✏ Let's Practice! ✏

# Daily Positive
# Affirmations Drawing

Draw a picture. Then write about your positive affirmation.

Name: ________________          Date: ________________

# ⭐ Daily Positive Affirmations ⭐
# Handwriting Practice

I am grateful for
my family.

✏️ Let's Practice! ✏️

# Daily Positive
# Affirmations Drawing

Draw a picture. Then write about your positive affirmation.

# Daily Positive Affirmations
# Handwriting Practice

I always do my
best.

 Let's Practice!

# Daily Positive Affirmations Drawing

Draw a picture. Then write about your positive affirmation.

# ★ Daily Positive Affirmations ★
## Handwriting Practice

I am important.

✏️ Let's Practice! ✏️

# Daily Positive
# Affirmations Drawing

Draw a picture. Then write about your positive affirmation.

# Daily Positive Affirmations
# Handwriting Practice

I am doing great things.

✏ Let's Practice! ✏

# Daily Positive
# Affirmations Drawing

Draw a picture. Then write about your positive affirmation.

Name: ___________________  Date: ___________________

# Daily Positive Affirmations Handwriting Practice

I am brave.

✏️ Let's Practice! ✏️

# Daily Positive Affirmations Drawing

Draw a picture. Then write about your positive affirmation.

Name: _______________     Date: _______________

# Daily Positive Affirmations
# Handwriting Practice

I am appreciated.

✏ Let's Practice! ✏

 # Daily Positive Affirmations Drawing 

Draw a picture. Then write about your positive affirmation.

# Daily Positive Affirmations
# Handwriting Practice

I am proud of
myself.

Let's Practice!

# Daily Positive
# Affirmations Drawing

Draw a picture. Then write about your positive affirmation.

Name:                              Date:

# Daily Positive Affirmations
# Handwriting Practice

I can learn anything
I set my mind to.

Let's Practice!

# Daily Positive
# Affirmations Drawing

Draw a picture. Then write about your positive affirmation.

Name: _______________     Date: _______________

# ✦ Daily Positive Affirmations ✦
## Handwriting Practice

I am an amazing

person.

✏️ Let's Practice! ✏️

 # Daily Positive Affirmations Drawing 

Draw a picture. Then write about your positive affirmation.

# Daily Positive Affirmations
# Handwriting Practice

Good things happen
to me.

 Let's Practice!

# Daily Positive
# Affirmations Drawing

Draw a picture. Then write about your positive affirmation.

# Daily Positive Affirmations
## Handwriting Practice

I am filled with
gratitude for the
abundance in my life.

Let's Practice!

# Daily Positive
# Affirmations Drawing

Draw a picture. Then write about your positive affirmation.

# ⭐ Daily Positive Affirmations ⭐
# Handwriting Practice

I am surrounded by positive and loving people.

 Let's Practice! 

# Daily Positive
# Affirmations Drawing

Draw a picture. Then write about your positive affirmation.

# ★ Daily Positive Affirmations ★
## Handwriting Practice

I am a good leader,
and my ideas inspire
others.

 Let's Practice! 

# Daily Positive Affirmations Drawing

Draw a picture. Then write about your positive affirmation.

# Daily Positive Affirmations
# Handwriting Practice

I am honest and
helpful.

 Let's Practice!

# Daily Positive
# Affirmations Drawing

Draw a picture. Then write about your positive affirmation.

# Daily Positive Affirmations
## Handwriting Practice

I am valued and my
opinion matters.

Let's Practice!

# Daily Positive
# Affirmations Drawing

Draw a picture. Then write about your positive affirmation.

# ⭐ Daily Positive Affirmations ⭐
## Handwriting Practice

I have the power to create anything I desire.

✏️ Let's Practice! ✏️

# Daily Positive
# Affirmations Drawing

Draw a picture. Then write about your positive affirmation.

# Daily Positive Affirmations
## Handwriting Practice

My life is fun and
filled with joy.

✏️ Let's Practice! ✏️

# Daily Positive
# Affirmations Drawing

Draw a picture. Then write about your positive affirmation.

# Daily Positive Affirmations Handwriting Practice

I am unique and special.

Let's Practice!

# Daily Positive
# Affirmations Drawing

Draw a picture. Then write about your positive affirmation.

# Daily Positive Affirmations Handwriting Practice

I am full of great
ideas and thoughts.

 Let's Practice!

# Daily Positive Affirmations Drawing

Draw a picture. Then write about your positive affirmation.

# ★ Daily Positive Affirmations ★
# Handwriting Practice

I am happy and at
peace.

✏️ Let's Practice! ✏️

# Daily Positive
# Affirmations Drawing

Draw a picture. Then write about your positive affirmation.

# ✦ Daily Positive Affirmations
# Handwriting Practice

I am patient with
myself as I learn
and grow.

✏ Let's Practice! ✏

# Daily Positive
# Affirmations Drawing

Draw a picture. Then write about your positive affirmation.

Name: ___________________     Date: ___________________

# Daily Positive Affirmations
# Handwriting Practice

I believe in myself

✏ Let's Practice! ✏

# Daily Positive
# Affirmations Drawing

Draw a picture. Then write about your positive affirmation.

# Daily Positive Affirmations
## Handwriting Practice

I am a good team
player and work
well with others.

✏ Let's Practice! ✏

# Daily Positive
# Affirmations Drawing

Draw a picture. Then write about your positive affirmation.

# Daily Positive Affirmations Handwriting Practice

I am constantly growing and improving.

## Let's Practice!

# Daily Positive
# Affirmations Drawing

Draw a picture. Then write about your positive affirmation.

# ★ Daily Positive Affirmations ★
# Handwriting Practice

I am worthy of
success.

✏ Let's Practice! ✏

Name: _______________________     Date: _______________________

 # Daily Positive Affirmations Drawing 

Draw a picture. Then write about your positive affirmation.

# Daily Positive Affirmations Handwriting Practice

I am loved for who
I am, not just for
what I do.

✏️ Let's Practice! ✏️

# Daily Positive Affirmations Drawing

Draw a picture. Then write about your positive affirmation.

# Daily Positive Affirmations Handwriting Practice

I am worthy of love, respect, and happiness.

Let's Practice!

# Daily Positive
# Affirmations Drawing

Draw a picture. Then write about your positive affirmation.

# Daily Positive Affirmations Handwriting Practice

I am kind and compassionate.

Let's Practice!

# Daily Positive
# Affirmations Drawing

Draw a picture. Then write about your positive affirmation.

# Daily Positive Affirmations
# Handwriting Practice

I am loved even on days when I feel down or sad.

✏️ Let's Practice! ✏️

# Daily Positive Affirmations Drawing

Draw a picture. Then write about your positive affirmation.

Name:                                    Date:

# Daily Positive Affirmations
# Handwriting Practice

I am a creative
thinker.

 Let's Practice! 

Name: ___________________    Date: ___________________

# Daily Positive Affirmations Drawing

Draw a picture. Then write about your positive affirmation.

81

Name:                Date:

# Daily Positive Affirmations
# Handwriting Practice

I am a bright light
in the world.

✏ Let's Practice! ✏

# Daily Positive Affirmations Drawing

Draw a picture. Then write about your positive affirmation.

Name: _______________          Date: _______________

# ★ Daily Positive Affirmations ★
## Handwriting Practice

I am a good
communicator.

✏ Let's Practice! ✏

# Daily Positive Affirmations Drawing

Draw a picture. Then write about your positive affirmation.

# Daily Positive Affirmations
## Handwriting Practice

I always find
creative solutions.

 Let's Practice! 

# Daily Positive Affirmations Drawing

Draw a picture. Then write about your positive affirmation.

Name: Date:

# Daily Positive Affirmations Handwriting Practice

I am full of courage
and face my fears
with bravery.

Let's Practice!

 # Daily Positive Affirmations Drawing 

Draw a picture. Then write about your positive affirmation.

Name: ___________________    Date: ___________________

# Daily Positive Affirmations
# Handwriting Practice

I am a good helper,
and my contributions
are valued.

✏️ Let's Practice! ✏️

# Daily Positive
# Affirmations Drawing

Draw a picture. Then write about your positive affirmation.

# Daily Positive Affirmations
# Handwriting Practice

I am loved and accepted for who I am, inside and out.

## Let's Practice!

# Daily Positive Affirmations Drawing

Draw a picture. Then write about your positive affirmation.

# ★ Daily Positive Affirmations ★
# Handwriting Practice

I am responsible.

✏️ Let's Practice! ✏️

# Daily Positive
# Affirmations Drawing

Draw a picture. Then write about your positive affirmation.

# Daily Positive Affirmations
# Handwriting Practice

I am a good role model, and others look up to me.

Let's Practice!

# Daily Positive
# Affirmations Drawing

Draw a picture. Then write about your positive affirmation.

# Daily Positive Affirmations
## Handwriting Practice

I contribute
positively to my
community.

Let's Practice!

Name: _______________________  Date: _______________________

 # Daily Positive Affirmations Drawing 

Draw a picture. Then write about your positive affirmation.

# Daily Positive Affirmations
# Handwriting Practice

I am mentally and
physically strong.

 Let's Practice!

Name: _______________          Date: _______________

# Daily Positive
# Affirmations Drawing

Draw a picture. Then write about your positive affirmation.

# Daily Positive Affirmations
# Handwriting Practice

I am a good sport,
and I celebrate
others' successes.

Let's Practice!

# Daily Positive
# Affirmations Drawing

Draw a picture. Then write about your positive affirmation.

Name:                                    Date:

# ✦✦ Daily Positive Affirmations ✦✦
# Handwriting Practice

I appreciate the
uniqueness of
others.

Let's Practice!

# Daily Positive
# Affirmations Drawing

Draw a picture. Then write about your positive affirmation.

# Daily Positive Affirmations
# Handwriting Practice

I am patient with
others as we learn
and grow.

✏️ Let's Practice! ✏️

# Daily Positive
# Affirmations Drawing

Draw a picture. Then write about your positive affirmation.

# Daily Positive Affirmations
# Handwriting Practice

I am honest and speak the truth with kindness.

## Let's Practice!

# Daily Positive
# Affirmations Drawing

Draw a picture. Then write about your positive affirmation.

# ★ Daily Positive Affirmations ★
# Handwriting Practice

I am strong, both
physically and
emotionally.

✏ Let's Practice! ✏

# Daily Positive
# Affirmations Drawing

Draw a picture. Then write about your positive affirmation.

# ⭐ Daily Positive Affirmations ⭐
# Handwriting Practice

I am mindful and I
focus on the
present moment.

✏️ Let's Practice! ✏️

# Daily Positive
# Affirmations Drawing

Draw a picture. Then write about your positive affirmation.

# Daily Positive Affirmations
# Handwriting Practice

I am generous, and
I enjoy giving to
others.

Let's Practice!

# Daily Positive Affirmations Drawing

Draw a picture. Then write about your positive affirmation.

# ✦ Daily Positive Affirmations ✦
# Handwriting Practice

I am loved by my
family and friends,
no matter what.

✏ Let's Practice! ✏

# Daily Positive Affirmations Drawing

Draw a picture. Then write about your positive affirmation.

# Daily Positive Affirmations
# Handwriting Practice

I am talented, and my skills bring joy to those around me.

✏️ Let's Practice! ✏️

# Daily Positive Affirmations Drawing

Draw a picture. Then write about your positive affirmation.

Name: Date:

# ★ Daily Positive Affirmations ★
## Handwriting Practice

I am resourceful
and find ways to
make things better.

Let's Practice!

# Daily Positive Affirmations Drawing

Draw a picture. Then write about your positive affirmation.

# ★ Daily Positive Affirmations ★
# Handwriting Practice

I am adaptable and
can adjust to
different situations.

✏️ Let's Practice! ✏️

# Daily Positive Affirmations Drawing

Draw a picture. Then write about your positive affirmation.

# ★ Daily Positive Affirmations ★
## Handwriting Practice

I am responsible for taking care of my body and mind.

## ✏ Let's Practice! ✏

# Daily Positive
# Affirmations Drawing

Draw a picture. Then write about your positive affirmation.

# ⭐ Daily Positive Affirmations ⭐
# Handwriting Practice

I am curious and
eager to learn.

✏️ Let's Practice! ✏️

# Daily Positive
# Affirmations Drawing

Draw a picture. Then write about your positive affirmation.

# Daily Positive Affirmations Handwriting Practice

I am in control of my thoughts, and I choose positivity.

## Let's Practice!

# Daily Positive
# Affirmations Drawing

Draw a picture. Then write about your positive affirmation.

# ⭐ Daily Positive Affirmations ⭐
# Handwriting Practice

I am beautiful inside
and out.

✏️ Let's Practice! ✏️

# Daily Positive Affirmations Drawing

Draw a picture. Then write about your positive affirmation.

# ★ Daily Positive Affirmations ★
# Handwriting Practice

I am capable of

overcoming

challenges.

✏️ Let's Practice! ✏️

 # Daily Positive
# Affirmations Drawing 

Draw a picture. Then write about your positive affirmation.

Name: ___________    Date: ___________

# ★ Daily Positive Affirmations ★
## Handwriting Practice

I am loved by
myself, my family,
and my friends.

✏️ Let's Practice! ✏️

# Daily Positive
# Affirmations Drawing

Draw a picture. Then write about your positive affirmation.

# ★ Daily Positive Affirmations ★
## Handwriting Practice

I am filled with love and share it with those around me.

✏️ Let's Practice! ✏️

Name: _______________    Date: _______________

# Daily Positive
# Affirmations Drawing

Draw a picture. Then write about your positive affirmation.

# Daily Positive Affirmations Handwriting Practice

Something good is happening for me today.

✏️ Let's Practice! ✏️

# Daily Positive
# Affirmations Drawing

Draw a picture. Then write about your positive affirmation.

# Daily Positive Affirmations
# Handwriting Practice

I am always in the
right place at the
right time.

✏️ Let's Practice! ✏️

# Daily Positive
# Affirmations Drawing

Draw a picture. Then write about your positive affirmation.

# Daily Positive Affirmations
# Handwriting Practice

I am a good planner,
and I organize my
tasks well.

## ✏️Let's Practice!✏️

# Daily Positive
# Affirmations Drawing

Draw a picture. Then write about your positive affirmation.

Name:                    Date:

# ★ Daily Positive Affirmations ★
# Handwriting Practice

☺ Write your own positive affirmation! ☺

I am a business owner.

✏ Let's Practice! ✏

# Daily Positive
# Affirmations Drawing

Draw a picture. Then write about your positive affirmation.

Name: ___________________  Date: ___________________

# ★ Daily Positive Affirmations ★
## Handwriting Practice

😊 Write your own positive affirmation! 😊

I am

✏️ Let's Practice! ✏️

# Daily Positive Affirmations Drawing

Draw a picture. Then write about your positive affirmation.

# Daily Positive Affirmations Handwriting Practice

☺ Write your own positive affirmation! ☺

I am

Let's Practice!

# Daily Positive
# Affirmations Drawing

Draw a picture. Then write about your positive affirmation.

# ★ Daily Positive Affirmations ★ Handwriting Practice

## 🙂 Write your own positive affirmation! 🙂

I am

✏️ Let's Practice! ✏️

# Daily Positive
# Affirmations Drawing

Draw a picture. Then write about your positive affirmation.

# Daily Positive Affirmations
# Handwriting Practice

 Write your own positive affirmation!

I am

✏ Let's Practice! ✏

# Daily Positive
# Affirmations Drawing

Draw a picture. Then write about your positive affirmation.

# Daily Positive Affirmations
# Handwriting Practice

☺ Write your own positive affirmation! ☺

I am ____________

✏ Let's Practice! ✏

# Daily Positive
# Affirmations Drawing

Draw a picture. Then write about your positive affirmation.

# Daily Positive Affirmations
# Handwriting Practice

🙂 Write your own positive affirmation! 🙂

I am

✏️ Let's Practice! ✏️

# Daily Positive
# Affirmations Drawing

Draw a picture. Then write about your positive affirmation.

Name: _______________    Date: _______________

# Daily Positive Affirmations
# Handwriting Practice

🙂 Write your own positive affirmation! 🙂

I am

✏️ Let's Practice! ✏️

# Daily Positive
# Affirmations Drawing

Draw a picture. Then write about your positive affirmation.

Name: _______________________     Date: _______________________

# Daily Positive Affirmations
# Handwriting Practice

☺ Write your own positive affirmation! ☺

I am

✏ Let's Practice! ✏

# Daily Positive
# Affirmations Drawing

Draw a picture. Then write about your positive affirmation.

Name: _______________     Date: _______________

# ⭐ Daily Positive Affirmations ⭐
# Handwriting Practice

🙂 Write your own positive affirmation! 🙂

I am

✏️ Let's Practice! ✏️

 # Daily Positive Affirmations Drawing 

Draw a picture. Then write about your positive affirmation.

☺ Write your own positive affirmation! ☺

I am

✏ Let's Practice! ✏

# Daily Positive
# Affirmations Drawing

Draw a picture. Then write about your positive affirmation.

www.ingramcontent.com/pod-product-compliance
Lightning Source LLC
Chambersburg PA
CBHW081400130726

47998CB00011B/3025